Making the Important Measurable,
Not the Measurable Important

With the international frenzy these days around assessment; with politicians jumping to numbers; the education world sorely needs a sensible, basic, powerful, accessible guide to authentic measurement. In 'Making the Important Measurable', Davidson and McEachen have given us a just-in-time guide to taking the right action that will help teachers, their students, and indeed society—actions that will actually improve as well as assess learning.

Michael Fullan
Professor Emeritus, OISE/University of Toronto

There is no greater imperative in the field of education assessment than finding an escape from the dominance of high-stakes, paper-and-pencil, multiple-choice tests. Davidson and McEachen have pointed out the path to freedom.

Gene Glass
Regents' Professor Emeritus, Arizona State University

Read the title and subtitle carefully. Give yourself a moment to take in what is being promised. This book delivers fully on the promise in the title -- and does so with insight, clarity, deep knowledge of the issues involved, methodological sophistication, cutting edge analysis, and actionable solutions. It just doesn't get any better than that.

Michael Quinn Patton
Author of Qualitative Research & Evaluation Methods, 4th ed

Making the Important Measurable, Not the Measurable Important

How Authentic Mixed Method Assessment helps unlock student potential – and tracks what really matters

E. Jane Davidson, Ph.D., and Joanne McEachen

the
learnerfirst
creating choice for children through education

Print Edition (March, 2015)
Also available as an e-book.

978-0692389591

0692389598

For information, please contact the publisher:

The Learner First™
Seattle, WA, USA
Joanne.m@thelearnerfirst.com
www.thelearnerfirst.com

Contents

Written by: E. Jane Davidson, Ph.D. and Joanne McEachen

Published by: The Learner First™, Seattle, WA, USA

March 2015

For more information about The Learner First™, visit www.TheLearnerFirst.com

Making the Important Measurable, Not the Measurable Important

How Authentic Mixed Method Assessment helps unlock student potential – and tracks what really matters

What if decisions about what to teach and how to teach put the learner first? What if we started with what the kids know and love, and helped them learn from there?

What if teachers really had their fingers on the pulse of how each learner was doing every day – doing real-time assessment of not just what's easy to measure, but what really matters? And what if that told them what the learner needed next?

What if "what really matters" was infused with who a learner was, what they loved, who they aspired to be, and what they needed to learn in order to get there?

What if that real-time assessment was based on the full range of evidence, qualitative and quantitative, that supported teachers to use sound professional judgment in a nuanced but consistent way?

And what would it look like if we could aggregate that evidence up to create a system-wide tracking framework that would show how well students, classrooms, schools, districts, and states were tracking relative to rich and meaningful targets?

With The Learner First™, these things are achievable, practical, and valid. The Learner First™ works at multiple levels of the system to effect deep and lasting change – and to leave behind the capabilities needed to build on that change.[1] Authentic Mixed Method Assessment is the tool for translating this worthy 'what if' thinking into an evidence-based, defensible reality.

---

1 Senge (2000)

Putting the Learner First

We all want kids to have the opportunity to be successful in their lives, and we want them to have all the right knowledge and skills that will allow them to get there. There is no argument about this in educational circles; the debate is generally around the best ways to achieve this.

This mini-book presents one important slice of a comprehensive and proven approach to accelerating student achievement. We call it The Learner First™ approach – and that's its central tenet.

The Learner First™ approach taps into the best knowledge and know-how available, from educational research and from real-world application and experience. It is grounded in a blend of pedagogical theories including humanistic, constructivist, transformational, and authentic.[2] The evidence base for these approaches provides a useful picture of what kinds of learning experiences affect cognitive, behavioral, and attitudinal outcomes.[3]

Our learner-centered approach to assessment, accelerated learning, and system-wide change has been woven together from these theoretical and empirical roots. It aligns easily with standards-based educational assessment and evaluation. But most importantly, it delivers real results for learners.

Core to The Learner First™ approach is working out what's most important for students and making that measurable and system-trackable, for both formative and summative purposes. It's not just a great assessment or outcome evaluation system; it's part of what helps shift thinking and practice at every level of the system.

The Learner First™ Authentic Mixed Method Assessment system not only helps teachers unlock potential in their learners; it provides rich, usable evidence of what's working in real time. That helps inform learning and teaching on an ongoing basis.

---

2 See Corneius-White, & Harbaugh. (2010); Shepard (2000); Weimer (2013); Newmann, Marks &, Gamoran (1996); and Wiggins (1990) for the individual treatment and integration of these pedagogies.
3 Cornelius-White (2007)

Commonly, there is a huge disconnect between this kind of meaningful formative assessment and summative tracking of student outcomes. Teachers may use a range of evidence to understand where a student is at and use that to inform their teaching. But, more often than not, system-wide tracking uses a single standardized assessment tool – whether it is norm-referenced or criterion-referenced – and that metric is treated like what "really" matters.

That disconnect creates disharmony between best practice in the classroom and how students, teachers, schools, and systems are deemed to pass or fail, be effective or ineffective.

The Curriculum and Pacing Guide Trap

Let's begin by talking about some of the traps and fishhooks in the current system, why they don't work, and what Authentic Mixed Method Assessment can offer as a genuine alternative.

There are good reasons behind creating well thought out curricula and putting them in the hands of every teacher in every classroom.[4] It helps ensure that every child is delivered the same quality product, and no one misses out on something critical. Pacing guides are intended to help ensure that the same content is delivered at the same pace.

Similarly, the most widely tracked assessment tools are designed to test the knowledge that the curriculum covers.

The rationale is to ensure that every learner is getting access to the same high quality content regardless of whom their teacher is or where they go to school. And, we have a consistent way of tracking learners' progress, no matter where they are in the system.

It does make perfect sense to outline a national or state curriculum. The problem is how this plays out in practice.

Curriculum is often treated like a highly prescriptive recipe for what to cover for every child in every classroom. It doesn't take into account who the students are, what is relevant for them, what they already know[5], or whether they even need to know some of the content. [6,7]

4 Darling-Hammond (2004)
5 Bernhardt (2010)
6 For a discussion of how educators should be drawing on pre-existing understandings and how this transfers to true integrated learning, see Bransford, Brown & Cocking (1999).
7 Fullan & Langworthy (2014)

Rethinking the Notion of Curriculum

What should a curriculum be, then? Ideally, it should be a deliberately broad guide of what learners in our country/state need in the way of skills and know how, in order to work with whatever content is relevant for them in their real worlds.

What does that look like in practice?

Math. Algebra. Geometry. These classes are so often taught in a way that is either completely abstract or applied only to an incredibly narrow set of examples that are of no relevance to most learners.

How would we approach Math, Algebra, and Geometry if we started with the learner first?

Suppose you started by finding out who the students were in your class, what interested them, and who they aspired to be. You may find students who are interested in pets, or building, or being a hair stylist, or a doctor, or an entrepreneur.

The next step is to find out what they already know. This may sound time-consuming, but it may surprise you – and in the end it will save both you and them a great deal of time. Some students will already know how to solve many algebraic or geometrical problems because they already do this at home, through their hobbies, in their after school jobs, or with friends.

... a deliberately broad guide of what learners in our country/state need in the way of skills and know how, in order to work with whatever content is relevant for them in their real worlds.

The key here is to look to the curriculum as a broad guide, but approach it in two ways: (1) individualized learning needs and (2) integration and relevance.[8]

First, start with what the students already know and teach from there. In other words, only deliver the parts of the curriculum that each of your students actually needs.[9] One size fits one.

Second, connect the learning experience to what they know and love, and allow them to develop their skills in that space.[10] That means having your builders calculate how much timber is needed to construct a shed; your hair stylists working out the volumes of hair color to mix for a certain client; your pet turtle enthusiasts calculating time, distance, and speed by racing their turtles down the school corridors; and the doctors working out the correct dose of Tylenol for a child of a certain weight.

Better yet, ask them to solve a real-world problem that hasn't been solved before and that will make a difference to their lives, utilizing algebra and geometry skills and concepts.[11]

But shouldn't we be using approaches that are evidence-based?

Naturally, teachers, leaders, and politicians prefer to see "proven" programs and strategies used in classrooms and schools. It makes sense, right?

The existing evidence base is important, but won't tell us the right approach for every individual. Every teacher still needs to use the evidence before their very eyes about what is working for every kid in their classroom.

---

8 McCombs (2000)
9 For a discussion of how a learner-centered perspective starts with understanding the needs and pre-existing knowledge base of each learner, see Fullan & Scott (2014), McCombs & Whistler (1997), and APA Work Group of the Board of Educational Affairs (1997).
10 McCombs & Miller (2007)
11 Fullan & Langworthy (2014)

We need to draw on the knowledge from evaluation and other empirical research, but we need to apply it thoughtfully, tailoring it to each individual learner, not implement a single approach right across the board. Even the strategies backed by really sound evidence still may not work for every single child.

What teachers see in everyday practice is evidence!

Teachers already are using evidence-based practice, if we take that term to mean what it actually does in the dictionary.

What every teacher sees before his or her eyes, when they watch how their students learn, what they respond to, what engages them, what helps them grasp concepts or create knowledge – all of this *is evidence!*

But here is the problem. Certain kinds of evidence – what teachers can see before their very eyes in real time as they watch their students learn – is for some reason (mistakenly) considered inferior and not trustworthy.

As education professionals, we have come to revere far narrower research conducted by an external person who may be thousands of miles from the kids we are trying to teach, has never even met one of them, knows nothing of their lives or their interests ... yet somehow this evidence from afar is considered the "real" evidence?

It's true that great evaluation and applied research is an important source to look to when trying to work out how to create the most powerful possible learning experiences for each child.

Just as doctors look to medical research for broad understandings but then tailor the treatment to the individual patient and their particular needs, so too every educator needs to tailor their approach for each learner in front of them.

In the real world of teaching, we need to look at each individual and work out: (a) which pieces of the knowledge base are going to be applicable for that student, and (b) which approach works best for that student.

This means taking into account not one or the other, but BOTH the insights that stream out from the research AND what appears before our eyes or is discussed in the staffroom.[12]

Teachers have to be great blenders and synthesizers of a wide range of information. It is fatal to lock into something narrow and treat it as a "truth" that trumps all else.[13]

In the real world of the classroom, we have to look across the full range, see what matters, see what's relevant, and work out the right blend to make a difference for the kid whose eyes we are looking into right this second.[14,15]

How do great educators do it? Knowledge. Synthesis. Know-how. Intuition.

The REAL truth is that the most amazing educators and educational leaders anywhere are not those who take "off-the-shelf" approaches and implement them strictly according to plan. They are skilled synthesizers of all kinds of information.

As practitioners, the vast knowledge they have gleaned from both formal sources and from their own experience have become so ubiquitous in their minds, so intuitive, that they often don't even know where their ideas come from any more. They just 'are'.

---

12 Fullan (2010); Weimer (2013)
13 See Davidson (2005), Mersman & Davidson (1999) for a discussion of synthesizing qualitative and quantitative data and the problems with giving one superiority over the other.
14 For a discussion of how assessments can and should relate to the student's world in a multilayered way, see Janesick (2006).
15 McEachen & Davidson (2014)

It's a true blend of knowledge and know-how – explicit (formal) knowledge and tacit (informal) knowledge[16]. Key point: tacit knowledge or know-how is *also* evidence in its own right.

But when a practitioner or leader like this is asked, "What is your evidence base?" they often find it difficult to answer. Not because their practice isn't based in evidence, but because the vast array of evidence has been filed away in *practical* file drawers inside their minds. And the way they apply it is now so seamless and intuitive that they are barely aware of how they do it.

The Learner First™ approach helps educators access this sound judgment in a cohesive and defensible way.

Assessing What Really Matters

What does really matter? And, is it the same for each learner?

As educators (e.g., teaching math), we need to have a broad understanding of each of our students' interests, aspirations, and learning needs. This helps us understand how best to create learning experiences that will engage them and give them the knowledge, skills, and competencies they need.

For example, we need to know:

Who is this student?

What is she interested in?

What does she need to know, or know how to do, in math?

What does she know already?

What does she need to learn next?

---

16 Polanyi (1966)

What topics, real-life applications, or approaches to learning are going to engage her and help her learn?

How can I, as a math teacher, use a broad range of assessment information to help me see the whole picture here?

Traditional assessment tools give us fine detail on particular knowledge and skills, but only tap into a small sample of the domain of what we need to know. Also, they tend to sample some pieces of the picture better than others (see figure 1).

Figure 1. Traditional assessment tools provide fine detail on particular knowledge and skills, but only on a small sample of the full domain of what we need to know.

The three pieces of traditional assessment data (depicted as the magnifying glasses in Figure 1) might give us a detailed view of *certain* aspects of this student's

- Understanding of math concepts
- Abstract, quantitative, and adaptive reasoning

- Mathematical problem solving skills
- Fluency in mathematical procedures

If the assessments used only multiple choice test formats (as is common), *they will only tell us those aspects of the above that lend themselves to this format of testing.*

Traditional math assessments would <u>not</u> tell us anything about:

- the student's ability to relate what she had learned to something in her own area of interest,
- how relevant she sees math to her life,
- her self-efficacy in math, or
- what special mathematical knowledge she might need to pursue her aspirations.

Using a Broader Mix of Evidence

Does this mean we need to create a huge array of assessment tools to cover the entire domain?

Not at all. That would be "paralysis by analysis".

The reality is that teachers already have at their fingertips a lot of the information they need to fill those gaps. Every single day, every teacher sees and observes how each student in their class works with math. They see homework and in-class assignments and learning tasks, and they get the chance to speak with students and their parents and families about the practical application of math at home and elsewhere.

These are the valuable pieces of information that put flesh on the bones of the [usually quantitative] measures[17] of achievement in math. They may be a little 'fuzzier', a little richer, a little harder to pin down with precision, but they are there, and they are important.

---

17 Fullan & Langworthy (2014)

Authentic mixed method assessment uses <u>all</u> the relevant evidence available about the student – *including* the traditional assessment results (depicted by the magnifying glasses in figure 2) but also the other things we see and hear, such as homework assignments, observations of in-class work, and conversations with the student and her parents.

Figure 2. Authentic mixed method assessment allows us to better 'see' the whole student. Only some of the evidence is fine-grained and not every detail is covered.

This other information may not be in such fine-grained detail as we get from formal assessment tools, but it does allow us to 'see' the whole student – who she is, what she knows, and what she needs – in enough detail to work out how to create learning experiences that will work for her.

Many teachers already use a range of evidence to understand where each student is at in their learning. They know instinctively (and are right) that this is the real truth about that student's achievement. It's a rich picture, not just one piece of evidence.[18]

---

18 The New Teachers Project (2013)

Test scores are part of the mix of what every teacher considers when assessing progress, but they are by no means the full picture.[19]

Doing Real-Time Assessment

It feels great to be organized. As a teacher, juggling so much, it feels good to have the lessons planned out weeks in advance.

But when teaching is truly responsive to learners' needs, it doesn't just mean tailoring the weeks-in-advance lesson plans; it means having your finger on the pulse of learning in real time, so you can deliver responsive, agile, real-time learning experiences.[20]

Real-time teaching needs real-time assessment. That means that every teacher knows every single day where every learner is at and what he or she needs to learn next. That means not needing to wait for the next standardized test results, but knowing what's happening right now. [21]

In this new context where you have students learning key concepts in different ways, at different paces, and applied to different real-world issues, how do you know when they have mastered a concept or competency?

It's one thing to have been able to successfully complete a learning task – something that is easily verifiable with observation. But to assess those deeper levels of learning, we have to ask probing questions to find out whether the student is aware of how they did things, can explain the reasoning, and so forth.

At the next level, you might ask them to draw out the general principles or concepts and apply them to another situation, explaining how and why they will work there too.

---

19 For more on how assessments may drive instead of serve educational goals, see Sergiovanni (2000).
20 Fullan & Langworthy (2014)
21 This is especially true for ongoing assessments for formative purposes. See Scriven (1967), Scriven (1991), and more recently Greenstein (2010)

In assessing all these different levels of learning, there are times when standardized tools will be useful and available, but many other times when they will not. You may need to design a quick assessment task yourself that taps into the key skills and understandings. You will *always* need to use your own professional judgment to assess understanding.

Whichever tools you use, the overarching purpose and principles are the same: know in real time how every student is doing in their learning. And real time literally means daily. What they have grasped today, what excited them today, gives you ideas for how you can make tomorrow an amazing learning day for them too.

Over the course of weeks or months, a teacher can build a rich picture of how a student is doing in various aspects of their learning. That's fine for informing what to do next on a day-to-day basis, but there is also a need to bring all this information up to a bigger-picture level.

Is this student on track to be successful in this subject area or competency?

Answering that question requires us to pull back and consider the multiple sources of evidence we have gathered over time, from observing performance on learning and assessment tasks, from assignments completed, tests taken, and conversations with students and their parents about how well they grasp the concepts and can apply them in the real world.

This is where Authentic Mixed Method Assessment tools really come into their own.

At any point in time, a teacher needs to know – and be able to clearly explain to a student and his or her parents/family – where he or she is overall in their progress, relative to what they need. Remember, this doesn't just mean relative to the State benchmarks on a particular assessment instrument; it means relative to the full range of knowledge, skills, and competencies the student needs in order to follow his or her aspirations.

A "progress snapshot" is important to have at your fingertips not just for each student, but for the class as a whole, so the teacher can see who will need more intensive help to accelerate them to where they should be.

How can a high-level assessment work if all the students are learning somewhat different things in different ways?

The key – as in The Learner First™ Authentic Mixed Method Assessment tools – is to create a broad, shared-language way of interpreting whatever evidence is relevant and available for each learner, but with enough consistency that it allows diverse learners' progress to be tracked on the same broad scale.

System-Wide Tracking

As we've already said, the key to designing highly effective and connected learning experiences is to look at the *whole picture* of who a student is, who they aspire to be, and what they need to learn, not just the narrow slice of it that happens to be measurable with the available tools.

Focusing on what's most easily measurable can lead teaching down a narrow path, and teachers are likely to miss what is really important for each student.

Sadly, what gets focused on at the system level (district, state, country) in tracking student achievement tends to be scores on a small subset of the standardized assessment tools a teacher uses – sometimes only one of them. In other words, just one or two of the magnifying glasses (see figure 1).

This creates a distraction for the teacher who is focusing in real time on what really matters, but their performance is tracked on something else. They end up "teaching to the test" instead of teaching what ignites each learner.

If an overall assessment using a range of mixed method evidence is the closest thing we have to a clear picture of where a student is at, why on earth would we track performance on anything else?

Here's why.

Even good mixed method assessment by teachers is not usually synthesized into anything that can be tracked across the system.

The real-time formative assessment that teachers do every day based on all the evidence they have at their fingertips is not captured in any trackable way, and so can't be aggregated up to get a school-wide or a system-wide picture of performance.

This is the breakthrough that has been needed for a long time: *Making the Important Measurable.*

> Tracking achievement using just one standardized test creates a distraction for the teacher who is focusing in real time on what really matters.
>
> They end up "teaching to the test" instead of teaching what ignites each learner.

Rob Neu – Superintendent Oklahoma City Public Schools has worked with The Learner First™ team for 3 years and adopted The Learners First™ framework for Whole System Change.

"I have truly been blessed to work with Jane (Davidson) and Joanne (McEachen) in applying the authentic mixed method of assessment. They show us how to put the needs of the learner first. By doing so, we are saving children from the academic death sentence of high stakes testing to authentic engagement. And we are transforming the lives of the educators who chose this profession to work with children, not prepare for standardized tests."

Robert Neu
Superintendent Oklahoma City Public Schools

The Learner First™ Authentic Mixed Method Assessment System

The Learner First™ Authentic Mixed Method Assessment System captures and tracks real, authentic teacher assessments in a meaningful and practical way. This, in turn, means that all levels of the system (students, parents, teachers, principals, district leaders) can now focus on the evidence that actually matters for each learner.

But aren't teacher judgments "just subjective"?

The biggest challenge here is that standardized assessment tools are seen as "objective" while qualitative evidence and teacher judgment are often viewed as "subjective" and "open to interpretation". But what does that mean, really?

The word "subjective" actually has several different meanings, and we need to be crystal clear about which are potentially problematic and which are not[22,23,24].

An accusation of "subjectivity" is usually an insinuation that the basis for evidence or a conclusion is highly personal or idiosyncratic. In other words, one person could draw a very different conclusion from another, therefore (the argument goes) the conclusion is no more than personal opinion and is certainly not a fact about performance or achievement.

There's something else about this that we need to keep very clear. Learning happens inside the mind, and is therefore an intrinsically subjective experience in its own right – in the exact same way as other 'mental events' are. Think of headaches, stress, happiness, enjoyment, love, motivation.

What if we ask a student how well they understand something? Is this "just subjective"? We are certainly asking them to talk about something important that they have directly experienced. Like a

---

22 Scriven (1991)
23 Davidson (2005)
24 Davidson (2012)

headache, there really IS no other way to understand how well they have grasped it[25].

In that sense, every "objective" standardized test is asking for understanding inside a student's mind, so does that make such tests "just subjective"?

Asking about subjectively-experienced events such as learning is a completely valid way of finding good evidence about learning. Sure, it's just one part of the picture, but it's an important piece of evidence that should not be dismissed offhand. It should be used alongside a multi-choice test, for example, and not be replaced by one.

The word "subjective" is also used as a derogatory term for any form of qualitative evidence. What's interesting about this is that every quantitative assessment item in a test is built from a qualitative understanding of the nature of the learning domain.

But somehow, once something is quantified (e.g., turned into a multiple-choice test item rather than an open-ended question or an observed learning task), it is somehow endowed with a higher "truth value".

There is another meaning of the term subjective, one that is very important to understand. "Subjective" also means "determined using a human brain rather than a machine or measuring device"[22].

For example, when a teacher grades a student essay, he or she uses professional judgment against a set of criteria for what constitutes a "good"

---

[25] Fullan & Langworthy (2013)

essay on this topic and at this particular level. Now, is essay grading "all just subjective" in the sense of being purely based on personal preferences and opinion?

No, it isn't.

With a well-designed grading guide (rubric), experienced teachers would come to largely similar conclusions about the quality of an essay, assigning it very similar grades.

Would there be small differences among teachers? Sure. But not to the extent where one says it's an outstanding essay and another says it's extremely poor.

This is the essential difference between professional judgment and personal opinion. The former can be clearly justified relative to criteria and a rubric that describe what an 'A' essay looks like, as opposed to a 'B', etc. The latter (personal opinion) can have no justification other than "I liked it" (or not).

There is a really important reality here too. There simply is no better way to judge the quality of an essay or a piece of student writing than using the brain of an experienced professional.

It's true that there are now computer algorithms that score essays based on pre-set algorithms, but these have important flaws.

Essay scoring algorithms key on the things that "indicate" quality is high (such as the use of complex sentence structures and sophisticated vocabulary), rather than going right to the core of what great writing really is. That's something only a human brain can do – at least for now!

What about the reliability and validity of Authentic Mixed Method Assessment?

In any and all assessment, validity (Are we measuring what we should be measuring – and are we measuring it right?) is the primary concern. Reliability (Are we measuring it in a stable/replicable way?) becomes important only after we have established validity.

The foundation for everything is construct validity, and more specifically content validity. Have we correctly defined "the construct" (i.e., the content or concept domain we should be measuring) and are we measuring that correctly?

"Defining the construct" is what we were referring to earlier when we discussed **Assessing What Really Matters** (p. 9). How do we define what "success" should look like for a particular learner?

We have argued that standardized tests sample content from some parts of the construct domain, but exclude large and important chunks of how "success" should actually be defined (see figure 1).

By definition, that points to weak content validity (which is the most fundamental part of construct validity).

Educational researchers will often conduct a range of other tests to determine the validity of assessment instruments. There are multiple ways of doing this[26], and one of the most common is convergent validity – seeing whether the assessment correlates highly with some other validated measure of the same construct.

Right now, the main assessment instruments that are considered to be "validated" are the very standardized tests we have just determined are inadequate because they don't cover enough content of the construct domain. They don't capture the full story. For that reason, to validate mixed method rubrics against them simply makes no sense!

---

[26] A fuller discussion of how to assess the reliability and validity of mixed method rubrics for assessment and evaluation will be presented in a forthcoming paper.

In Authentic Mixed Method Assessment, we are asking educators to draw on a wide range of evidence that *includes* standardized test scores but takes into account *so much more* (see p. 9).

If rubric-based judgments were very highly correlated with standardized test scores (which many would say was high convergent validity), that would actually mean that teachers were considering very little else apart from those standardized test scores! In other words, they wouldn't be synthesizing the full range of evidence in order to best activate learning.

The bottom line is this. The validity of Authentic Mixed Method Assessment rubrics is primarily determined by how well they define what "success" really should look like for each learner.

How do we do that? We start with a broad definition for the specific groups of learners learning within a particular system (e.g., district, cluster, or school). That definition is informed by federal/national and state expectations, but also by a knowledge of who our learners are.

Second, we write the descriptors at each level so that they are not overly specific and can therefore be interpreted appropriately for each individual child. For example, "success in literacy" for a bilingual child means being able to read and write in *both* of their languages, not just one. For a child who is passionate about electricity, it means mastering the vocabulary of that topic area as well as the general vocabulary needed for everyday life.

There is a lot more to this validity discussion than meets the eye, and we certainly plan to cover it off in more depth in a future paper. However, we hope that the above brief explanation helps to lay out some of the key points that are important to an educator.

What can we do to ensure reliability of ratings?

One pressing practical concern with the use of rubric-based judgments is the question of interrater reliability. When teachers are beginning to use a new tool like this, there will be a learning curve as they 'calibrate' their thinking and judgment against others.

How do we maximize the reliability of a teacher's professional judgment, so that there is better agreement among teachers grading an essay? We start by having a clearly defined grading guide, or rubric. This provides a shared language and a shared understanding of how performance is defined at different levels.

Rating consistency can also be improved with a formal moderation process, where a sample of student achievement ratings is cross-checked independently. The learning conversations that teachers have around this process are also valuable for understanding where student achievement is strong and weak, why this is so, and what works to shift it.

We can also get more valid, reliable ratings by assessing performance on not just a single essay or assignment, but overall achievement in a subject area, based on the full range of evidence about what really matters. Our experience is that interpretation of a single piece of evidence tends to vary more among raters than assessment of a body of evidence.

In the assessment of student progress and achievement (as opposed to their performance on a particular piece of work), it is important to have clear and valid guidelines showing what the full mix of assessment evidence would look like at high, adequate, and low levels of performance. This encourages teachers to consider the available evidence as a set (which they would hopefully be doing as part of formative assessment, so that they know what to do next).

The fact that the system takes a while to calibrate initially is no reason to call it unreliable or "just subjective". It still provides a very good and defensible answer to the important question of how a student is doing overall; based on *all* the best evidence we have available.

The Learner First™ System in Practice

The Learner First™'s rubric-based judgment approach to mixed method assessment helps schools and districts finally produce and learn from evidence that captures what is most important. It converts rich information into a trackable metric that looks simple, but isn't a narrow oversimplification of what is important about achievement in a particular area.

To see what this rubric-based mixed method approach actually looks like, here is an example from a Math target we tracked within one school district:

> **Target:** 100% of our African American, Pacific Islander, and Latino boys in Grades 3, 5, 8, &10 will: (a) see math as relevant and meaningful for their lives, now and in their futures and (b) be achieving at or above standard in math by the end of the school year.

Note that the target wasn't simply about performance on a single test, but it was on seeing both relevance and success in Math (see Figure 4).

Student progress against this target was tracked using up to seven pieces of evidence, which teachers considered as a set, coming to overall ratings on a 5-point scale (see Table 1).

One key to the tool is that it is designed to track accelerations and slip-backs, rather than standard progress for one academic year. If a student starts the year "well on track" and makes the standard amount of progress for the year, he or she will finish the year at the same rating, well on track.

Table 1. The Learner First™ 5-point rating scale for assessing how well students were seeing relevance and success in Math at any point in the year, and at any grade level.

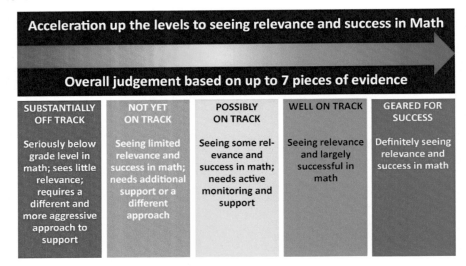

SUBSTANTIALLY OFF TRACK	NOT YET ON TRACK	POSSIBLY ON TRACK	WELL ON TRACK	GEARED FOR SUCCESS
Seriously below grade level in math; sees little relevance; requires a different and more aggressive approach to support	Seeing limited relevance and success in math; needs additional support or a different approach	Seeing some relevance and success in math; needs active monitoring and support	Seeing relevance and largely successful in math	Definitely seeing relevance and success in math

For any particular student, "success" is being in the green zone, well on track or geared for success. Students below those levels needed to not just make standard progress (which would keep them at the same rating); they needed to accelerate by moving up the levels, achieving more than a year's progress in one school year.

A good guide for rating progress covers much more than the broad descriptions in Table 1, which provide only a high-level view of the meanings of terms.

Teachers used the more detailed rubric shown in Table 2, which explains in much more specific terms what the constellation of evidence would look like for each learner on a wide range of evidence, including: STAR, Smarter Balance, End of Course assessments, The Learner First™ Relevance of Math Survey, Conversations and interviews with students and parents, and teacher observations.

Each teacher used whatever assessment evidence was available to him or her at the time of doing the rating.

Table 2. The Learner First™ Rubric for "Seeing Relevance and Success in Math"

Progress Rating	Performance Picture (description of evidence)
GEARED FOR SUCCESS Definitely seeing relevance and success in math	• Clearly achieving at or above standard in math for this point in the year (overall teacher judgment based on student coursework, in-class assessments, teacher observation, standardized tests, conversations and interviews with students) • Sees math as relevant and meaningful for his or her life, now and in the future. This is evident not just in reported attitudes (high scores on The Learner First™ Relevance of Math Survey Tool), but also evidence that math skills are actively and usefully applied to everyday life, even outside the classroom (e.g. as reported or observed by parents, students, and others)
WELL ON TRACK Seeing relevance and largely successful in math	• Achieving at standard in math, or very close to it, for this point in the year (overall teacher judgment based on student coursework, in-class assessments, teacher observation, standardized tests, conversations and interviews with students) • Generally sees math as relevant and meaningful for his or her life, now and in the future. This is evident not just in reported attitudes (relatively high scores on The Learner First™ Relevance of Math Survey Tool), but also evidence that math skills are applied to everyday life, even outside the classroom (e.g. as reported or observed by parents, students, and others)

Progress Rating	Performance Picture (description of evidence)
POSSIBLY ON TRACK Seeing some relevance and success in math; needs active monitoring and support	• Close to achieving at standard in math for this point in the year, although with some areas of weakness (overall teacher judgment based on student coursework, in-class assessments, teacher observation, standardized tests, conversations and interviews with students) • Starting to see math as relevant for his or her life. This is evident not just in reported attitudes (moderate scores on The Learner First™ Relevance of Math Survey Tool), but also some emerging evidence that math skills are starting to be applied to everyday life (e.g. as reported or observed by parents, students, and others)
NOT YET ON TRACK Seeing limited relevance and success in math; needs additional support or a different approach	• Well short of achieving at standard in math for this point in the year, with some significant areas of weakness (overall teacher judgment based on student coursework, in-class assessments, teacher observation, standardized tests, conversations and interviews with students) • Very limited view of math as relevant for his or her life. This is evident not just in reported attitudes (relatively low scores on The Learner First™ Relevance of Math Survey Tool), and very little evidence that math skills are applied to everyday life (e.g. as reported or observed by parents, students, and others)
SUBSTANTIALLY OFF TRACK Seriously below grade level in math; sees little relevance; requires a different and more aggressive approach to support	• Seriously below standard in math for this point in the year (overall teacher judgment based on student coursework, in-class assessments, teacher observation, standardized tests, conversations and interviews with students) • At this level, the student sees little or no relevance of math for his or her life. This is evident not just in reported attitudes (very low scores on The Learner First™ Relevance of math Survey Tool), and virtually no evidence that math skills are applied to everyday life (e.g. as reported or observed by parents, students, and others)

As mentioned earlier, a key feature of this rubric is that it tracks student achievement relative to where they should be at any particular time. A student who stays at the same level may well be progressing in their learning, but is not accelerating up the levels to get on track.

To move into a higher rating level (towards, into, or within the 'green zone' – which is where every learner needs to be), a student would need to make more than a year's progress within the school year.

The rating system provides user-friendly information for people at all levels of the system:

- For students (and their parents), it can make clearer what they are trying to achieve, which makes it easier for them to engage in meaningful conversations about what's important to them and how to get there.

- Parents and families can get a succinct gauge of how on track the student is, without waiting for the end-of-semester grade.

- Teachers can see 'at a glance' how the entire class is doing overall, without having to look across multiple assessments each time.

- School principals, District and State leaders can see in real time how achievement is tracking for particular target groups, or overall, so that they know sooner rather than later whether they need to adjust programs and approaches to get better results.

Figure 3 shows an example of how one middle school tracked in accelerating their 35 African American, Latino, and Pacific Island 8th grade boys in Math within one school year (see Figure 4).

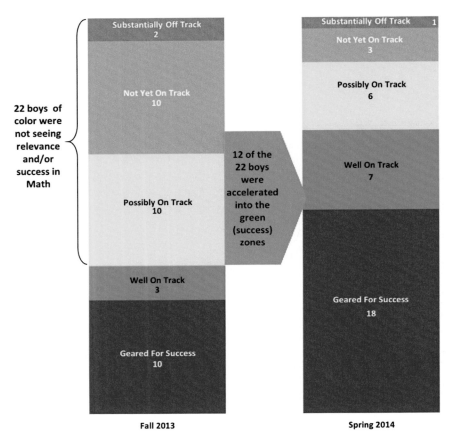

Fall 2013   **Spring 2014**

Figure 3. Accelerating 8th grade boys of color in seeing relevance and success in math

As we can see, more than half of the 22 boys initially not succeeding were accelerated (in both achievement and relevance) into the green zones ("Well on Track" or better).

This was more success than the school had been anticipating at the outset. Indeed, some stakeholders were skeptical that the results were real. But those who worked personally with these boys had seen the progress with their own eyes – and the standardized test score data mirrored their observations.

Many educators we work with are initially concerned that The Learner First™'s laser-like focus on very specific groups of focus students means that others outside those groups are missing out.

This means it's important to track not just the focus students, but *all* students in the grades covered by the targets. We do this to ensure that other groups of students are not seeing adverse (or, zero) effects. This is always important with targeted programs.

Looking at the results for the same middle school, large accelerations were evident even for those 8th grade boys who weren't part of the target (see Figure 4).

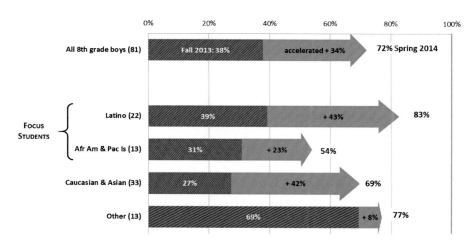

Figure 4. Matched pre-post data from one Learner First middle school, showing baseline and 1-year acceleration of both target and non-target boys into the math "green zone"

Of course, the target in question only covered boys of color – *but what about the girls in the same grades?* None of them were part of the target at all.

As Figure 5 shows, 8th grade girls at this school showed results as strong as the boys – despite not even being part of the target.

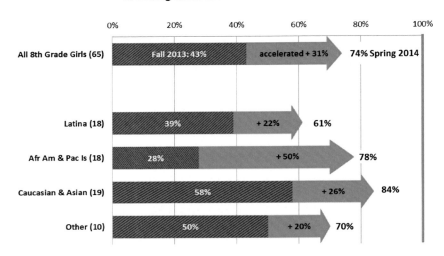

8th Grade Girls "Well on Track" or "Geared for Success" in Seeing Relevance & Success in Math

Figure 5. Matched pre-post data from one Learner First middle school, showing baseline and 1-year acceleration of 8th grade girls (who were not in the target group at all) into the math "green zone"

But why does it work for learners we weren't even targeting?

Two reasons.

What you measure becomes what you do. One of the amazing shifts in conversation we noticed as schools started using The Learner First™ Authentic Mixed Method Assessment system was this:

Before: "Standardized test scores are low, so let's teach students how to score higher on the tests."

Now: "These students are still rated low on seeing relevance and success in math, so let's find a way to make learning experiences more relevant to them so they can better understand (and see the point of) math concepts."

Authentic assessment becomes a way of seeing that you can't 'unsee'. The Learner First™ framework for Authentic Mixed Method Assessment pushes teachers to truly focus on individual students – who they are, what they love, who they aspire to be, what they know already, and what ignites their learning.

We only ask teachers to do this intensively for a small number of target students – in this case, perhaps seven or eight boys in an 8th grade class of 30 students. But once you learn this way of truly seeing the person as an individual, you can't 'unsee' it.

In our experience, teachers who work like this with a small number of focus students end up starting to wonder who each of their other students are, what interests him or her, and what will ignite their learning.

It causes a deep but subtle mind-shift, and that shifts behavior in amazing ways.

When the entire system around the teacher is also, at the same time, aligning with this new way of thinking about and working with students, it simply becomes natural, obvious, the right thing to do. It becomes "the way we do things around here."

Once educators see the kinds of results they always dreamed of helping their learners achieve – and when leaders see it truly "moving the needle" right across the system – the change becomes unstoppable.

What you measure becomes what you do.

Authentic assessment becomes a way of seeing that you can't 'unsee'.

The Learner First™ system is a powerful way to create real-time Authentic Mixed Method Assessment data that is trackable and easy to understand even at the whole-system level, despite the fact that it is based on a rich mix of evidence, both qualitative and quantitative.

Contrast this with what is usually done – taking just one of those assessment metrics and showing the results on that narrow measure, as though it is "*the* answer" to the question of how well learners (and schools, and Districts, and States, and countries) are doing.

On a rich and meaningful target such as this, which includes not just achievement but also seeing the relevance of Math, there is simply *no way* a single assessment tool can capture anywhere near the whole truth about performance.

But in reality, this is done again and again. Teachers are expected to assess on a wide range of evidence for formative purposes, but then the system tells them that the only thing that *really* counts is just one or two of those metrics. It's not surprising we get "teaching to the test" and many other unfortunate side effects of an outcome-tracking system that is overly narrow.

A system like this can help make the important measurable, and turn it into user-friendly snapshots (like the graphs shown earlier) that allow everyone to clearly see and celebrate dramatic progress among the students who most needed it. Better still, people at every level of the system know that underlying this easy-to-grasp evidence is a rich mix of evidence.

More importantly for students, a system like this enables and encourages teachers to think in a more rich and nuanced way about who their students are, what they need, and how to get them there.

When this kind of thinking is infused into outcome capture

and tracking all the way up the system, what's important is clear, and the incentives are in alignment, not out of kilter.

Ignite Your State, District, or School

Are you interested in hearing more about how your state, district, or school can make the important measurable and use Authentic Mixed Method Assessment to catalyze, track, and celebrate genuine accelerations in student achievement?

We can help you ignite potential and make the faces of your students, their parents, their teachers, and your leaders light up when they see what they can do.

Success for us is when you not only see and believe what is happening, but you know you have the tools, the know-how, and the passion to make it happen over and over.

Get in touch if you want to ignite your state, district or school:

E. Jane Davidson, Ph.D.
Chief Data Whisperer
The Learner First™
jane@TheLearnerFirst.com
Visit www.TheLearnerFirst.com

Joanne McEachen
Chief Destiny Changer
The Learner First™
joanne@TheLearnerFirst.com

About the authors

Dr. E. Jane Davidson

 As Co-founder and Chief Data Whisperer at The Learner First™, Jane uses practical educational, systems change, and evaluative know-how to create and track genuine deep change in education systems, states, districts, and schools.

An internationally recognized evaluation specialist and thought leader, Jane is best known for developing evaluation rubrics as a methodology for drawing conclusions about quality and value. She has also made significant contributions in the areas of causal inference for qualitative and mixed methods, and in synthesis methodologies for evaluation. She was 2005 recipient of the American Evaluation Association's prestigious Marcia Guttentag Award.

Jane is sought after as a speaker and top-level consultant for her signature approach of methodologically robust but refreshingly practical evaluation with breathtaking clarity. She has presented keynotes and invited workshops in the United States, Canada, the United Kingdom, Singapore, Brazil, South Africa, Australia, and New Zealand. Jane has facilitated successful workshops for AEA, CES, EES, AES, TEI, ANZEA, and UNISA, and coauthors a popular blog with another top international evaluator, Professor Patricia Rogers, at http://GenuineEvaluation.com.

Jane's text, *Evaluation Methodology Basics: The nuts and bolts of sound evaluation* (2005, Sage), has sold heavily in both the US and internationally as a graduate text and practitioner guidebook. Her mini-book, *Actionable Evaluation Basics: Getting succinct answers to the most important questions* (2012, Real Evaluation) is also available in Spanish and French.

After being recruited by Daniel Stufflebeam to serve as Associate Director of the internationally recognized Evaluation Center at Western Michigan University, Jane launched and directed the world's first fully interdisciplinary Ph.D. in Evaluation.

Prior to completing her doctorate at Claremont Graduate University (with Michael Scriven), Jane worked in training and development, quality assurance, and HR. She is also a qualified high school teacher of physics, chemistry, and science; and taught English in Japan for four years.

Joanne McEachen

President and Chief Destiny Changer of The Learner First™, a world-class education consulting and capacity building business based in Seattle, WA.

Joanne is an internationally recognized whole system education change leader; originally from New Zealand. She co-founded The Learner First™, where Joanne unashamedly focuses, inspires and motivates learners, parents, educators, communities and system leaders to put The Learner First™ and dramatically lift the performance of education systems to accelerate exactly the learners that have been left behind.

Joanne also serves as New Measures Director for New Pedagogies for Deep Learning: A Global Partnership. This multi-country, 1000-school initiative includes countries such as Finland, Australia, Uruguay, New Zealand, The Netherlands, Canada, and the USA.

Drawing on her deep expertise in creating change at every level of the K-12 system, Joanne has delivered numerous keynote addresses and professional learning labs to educators internationally from the USA, UK, Canada, Hong Kong, Uruguay, Finland, Australia, and New Zealand, on topics such as; Whole System Change, Educational Leadership, Authentic Assessment, Creating New Measures for Education Systems and Educational Technology.

Prior to immigrating to the United States, Joanne worked at every level of the education system from classroom teacher, to principal, to regional manager (superintendent), to leading several whole-country change initiatives. Within these roles she was responsible for the performance and outcomes of up to 2600 schools.

Joanne is best known for her leadership in the design and implementation of a major national (Federal Government level) system realignment for the Ministry of Education in New Zealand. This multi-pronged approach included targeted change management assistance for schools, a redesign of the system for funding and allocating professional development, and the redesign of PLCs as school cluster Learning and Change Networks.

References

APA Work Group of the Board of Educational Affairs (1997). *Learner-centered psychological principles: A framework for school reform and redesign*. Washington, DC: American Psychological Association.

Bernhardt, E. B. (2010). Teaching other languages. In H. J. W. Walberg & S. J. Paik (Eds.) *Educational practices series* (20). International Academy of Education and International Bureau of Education. Retrieved from: http://www.ibe.unesco.org/fileadmin/user_upload/Publications/Educational_Practices/EdPractices_20.pdf

Bransford, J. D., Brown, A. L., & Cocking, R. R. (Eds.) (1999). *How people learn: brain, mind, experience, and school*. Washington, DC: National Academy Press.

National Governors Association Center for Best Practices & Council of Chief State School Officers. (2010). *Common Core State Standards*. Washington, DC: Authors. Retrieved from: http://ww.corestandards.org

Cornelius-White, J. D., Cornelius-White J. H., & Harbaugh, A. P. (2010). *Learner-centered instruction: building relationships for student success*. Thousand Oaks, CA: Sage.

Cornelius-White, J. (2007). Learner-centered teacher-student relationships are effective: A meta-analysis. Review of Educational Research, 77; 113 143.

Darling-Hammond, L. (2004). Standards, accountability and school reform. *The Teachers College Record, 106*(6), 1047–1085.

Davidson, E. J. (2005). *Evaluation methodology basics: The nuts and bolts of sound evaluation*. Thousand Oaks, CA: Sage.

Davidson, E. J. (2012). *Actionable Evaluation Basics: Getting succinct answers to the most important questions*. Auckland, New Zealand: Real Evaluation.

Fullan, M. (2010). The big ideas behind whole system reform. *Education Canada, 50*(3), 24-27.

Fullan, M. & Langworthy, M. (2013). *Towards a new end: new pedagogies for deep learning*. White Paper published by Collaborative Impact SPC, Seattle, Washington.

Fullan, M., & Langworthy, M. (2014). *A rich seam: how new pedagogies find deep learning*. London: Pearson.

Fullan, M. & Scott, J. (2014). *Education PLUS: The world will be led by people you can count on, including you!* New Pedagogies for Deep Learning White Paper Published by: Collaborative Impact SPC, Seattle, Washington.

Greenstein, L. (2010). *What teachers really need to know about formative assessment*. Alexandria: VA: Association for Supervision & Curriculum Development.

Janesick V: J. (2006). *Authentic assessment primer*. New York, NY: Peter Lang Publishing, Inc.

McCombs, B. L., & Miller, L. (2007). *Learner-centered classroom practices and assessments*. Thousand Oaks, CA: Corwin Press.

McCombs, B., & Whistler, J. S. (1997). *The learner-centered classroom and school: strategies for increasing student motivation and achievement*. San Francisco, CA: Jossey-Bass Publishers.

McCombs, B. L. (2000). The learner-centered psychological principles excerpt from *Assessing the Role of Educational Technology in the Teaching and Learning Process: A Learner-Centered Perspective*. Retrieved from: http://www.ed.gov/rschstat/eval/tech/techconf00/mccombs_paper.html

McEachen, J., & Davidson, E. J. (2014). *Bringing deep learning to life-the story behind the development of the suite of tools for new pedagogies for deep learning: a global partnership*. White Paper published by Collaborative Impact SPC, Seattle, Washington.

Mersman, J. L. & Davidson, E. J. (1999, November). *Synthesizing qualitative and quantitative data: Simplicity and validity*. Paper presented at the meeting of the American Evaluation Association, Orlando, FL.

Newmann, F. M., Marks, M. H. &, Gamoran, A. (1996). Authentic pedagogy and student performance. *American Journal of Education 104*(4), 280-312.

Polanyi, M. (1966). *The tacit dimension*. Chicago, IL: University of Chicago Press.

Scriven, M. (1967). The methodology of evaluation. In R. W. Tyler, R. M. Gagné, & M. Scriven (Eds.), *Perspectives of curriculum evaluation* (pp. 39–83). Chicago, IL: Rand McNally.

Scriven, M., (1991). *Evaluation thesaurus* (4th ed.). Thousand Oaks, CA: Sage.

Sergiovanni, T. J. (2000). *The lifeworld of leadership: creating culture, community, and personal meaning in our schools*. San Francisco, CA: Jossey-Bass.

Senge, P. (2000). *Schools that learn: A fifth discipline fieldbook for educators, parents, and everyone who cares about education*. New York, NY: Doubleday.

Shepard, L. A. (2000). The role of assessment in a learning culture. *Educational Researcher, 29*(7), 4–14.

The New Teachers Project (2013). Perspectives of irreplaceable teachers: what America's best teachers think about teaching. Retrieved from [TNTP http://tntp.org/assets/documents/TNTP_Perspectives_2013.pdf]

Weimer, M. (2013). *Learner-centered teaching: five key changes to practice*. (2nd ed.). San Francisco, CA: Jossey-Bass.

Wiggins, G. (1990). The case for authentic assessment. *Practical Assessment, Research & Evaluation, 2*(2). Retrieved from: http://ericae.net/edo/ED328611.htm

Also by Davidson and McEachen:

8 Must Ask Questions to Get the Best Education for YOUR Child

Joanne McEachen and E. Jane Davidson, Phd.

New Pedagogies for Deep Learning Narrative

Bringing Deep Learning to Life - The story behind the development of the Suite of Tools for New Pedagogies for Deep Learning: A Global Partnership

Authors: Joanne McEachen and Jane Davidson, Ph.D.

Published by: Collaborative Impact SPC, Seattle, Washington

July 2014

For more information about New Pedagogies for Deep Learning visit www.newpedagogies.org.

EVALUATION METHODOLOGY BASICS

THE NUTS
AND BOLTS
OF SOUND
EVALUATION

E. JANE DAVIDSON

actionable
evaluation

basics

Getting succinct answers to
the most important questions

E. Jane Davidson, Ph.D.

Also available in: French and Spanish

20133171R00029

Made in the USA
San Bernardino, CA
28 March 2015